To Ron &

Best Wishes!

Jerilyn Minerva

# The CHRISTMAS Angel

# The CHRISTMAS Angel

A TRUE STORY

*Jerilyn Minerva*

STRATFORD
BOOKS

Front Cover photo includes Chrissy as described by author throughout the text.

Cover Design: Vance Hawkins
Book Cover Photography: Stan MacBean

ISBN: 0-929753-02-X
The Christmas Angel

Stratford Books
4308 37th Road North
Arlington, Virginia 22207

First Printing: August, 2000

This book is printed on acid-free paper.

Printed in the United States of America

*For my dear Aunt LaRee –*
*who treasured all children.*
*You taught me how to love . . .*

# ACKNOWLEGEMENT

Sharing this story seemed infinitely more important than ignoring it, and so I began, then began again – several times. Completing the project would have been impossible without the support of some really terrific people.

**Grateful appreciation goes to:**

Mother, who convinced me I can do anything that I put my mind to, and Daddy, who really *believes* that I can. You both gave me a great love of words, music and dancing – all miracles of expression. And you let me read when I should have been doing my chores. Without your strength, and your constant belief in me, I could not have written this story.

Deidra, my dear daughter, you are a great example to us all, and the love of my life. Thank you for listening to my stories, assuring me they were good enough to write, reassuring me they were good enough to read, pushing me to submit them, loving me unconditionally, and for picking me to be your mommy.

Jeff, for being a really great son-in-law and substitute dad to my grandchildren and to my second group of children, a terrific big brother, a kind and loving husband to my Deidra, and for writing the most exquisite poetry.

My little sister, Wendy — thank you for being there when no one else was, for taking your turns with my Chrismiss, and for loving my children, no matter where they came from.

Renae – my big sister, confidant, friend — thank you for loving me again, not leaving without me, propping me up, and for buying me bread pudding to celebrate.

My friends: SandraSue, for telling me I could, when I said I couldn't, and for reminding me that this writing business is my dream; Craig Lock, my church leader, who knew I was writing, didn't advise me to give it all up, and for caring for us all; Zappa, the first to know, you convinced me I was having fun; Heather, for rescuing the girls at the 11th hour, and helping me proofread. Thanks Sandy and Dennis for taking my girls to eat ice-cream so I could write, and then making me go so I would take a moment for myself. Thanks SR II for being the best … the absolute best.

Richard – thank you, for believing in this project, and giving me the courage to believe in myself. Somebody pinch me!

Most of all, thanks to my awesome children, who know I write about them – and thanks for letting me share your stories.

# PREFACE

I belong to an on-line group of MAV driving, bread baking, question asking, advice giving, opining SAHMS. We are Stay At Home Mommies. Let me explain my position on the phrase — *Stay at home mommy*. I am one, but I haven't always been. I worked when I was married, managing my life and children with day-care and time off during vacations. I am neither for, nor against working mommies. I think it's wonderful if you've worked hard to have a career and enjoy what you're doing. If you work because you have to, know that I've been there too. I also applaud your decision to stay at home whatever lead you to that choice. Families come in many flavors and mine is certainly a perfect example of that.

The SAHMs got into a Q & A session about miscarriages and what happens to the spirit of the unborn child. The catalyst for this discussion was: Deciding to not have any more children or having a medical condition that prevents having more children and how some people might feel there is someone missing in their family — another little spirit that just hasn't made it to the family. Some women who experience miscarriages, myself included, believe we will raise those children in heaven or perhaps find another way to raise other children. Miscarriage or the decision to limit one's family due to medical or other conditions is one that often tears at the very core of our existence. My personal philosophy is that each family has to decide the best course to travel.

I've felt for years that I was going to have more children — even more than the ones I'm adopting now, and not the children I've raised as step-children. I don't know how I'll get them or where they are today, and I might not get them until we're all together in Heaven (I'm the Eternal Optimist, here!).

*Challenging life at full speed*
*Winsome smile from ear to ear*
*A true brave heart — courageous love*
*Ability to soar on eagles' wings*

*Strength helps to conquer*
*Nothing but love to share with all*
*This daughter of Heavenly Father*
*Holds hope for us all*

—Jeffrey S. Knierim

# THE CHRISTMAS ANGEL
### *A True Story*

"She's here, Mom," whispered my daughter, Debbie, into the phone. "We picked her up at 5:00 o'clock. Her name is Crystal."

I glanced up at the mauve circle of time noted each hour by small green cacti. Almost 7 P.M. Rob and Debbie must have been back home from SeaTac Airport near Tacoma for nearly an hour. "I'm glad you beat the snow home, Honey."

The North wind cut a frozen path through the fir trees standing guard around my tiny cabin, and the air was growing colder, the clouds becoming dark and sinister. I reached up to check for drafts slicing through the double-pane window above the kitchen sink. There wasn't anything friendly about the skies tonight. The cactus clock had moved to Seattle with me from Tucson, Arizona, and was as much in contrast with this weather as I was.

"Yes, well . . . there's a problem." With Debbie and Rob there was always a problem. She was sunshine, he was ominous weather. She was water, he was oil. Debbie was soft, Rob was harsh. I didn't like him. Not from the moment she brought him home. In their case opposites *didn't* attract. He knew she was meek enough to control.

"Problem? Have you looked outside lately? Blizzard for sure tonight. How is she?" I wanted to ask so many questions. Does she look like Rob? Does she have things to wear in this weather? Is she happy? Sad? Confused? I still can't imagine anyone sending a child away this close to Christmas. I couldn't imagine anyone sending a five-year-old away at *anytime* of the year.

"Mom, can you come over right away? Crystal's not too happy. She left her coat on the plane and Rob won't get her another one and he won't let me call the airport to see if it's in lost and found. He said it was her punishment for being so careless. She won't let either one of us touch her, not even to hold her hand."

I could hear the frustration in Debbie's voice. Pulling the brown wool sweater tighter around my shoulders didn't help. There was no warmth to be found, not in a sweater, blanket or thought when I pictured Rob. He fancied himself a biker, but he wasn't near as nice.

I bit my lip until it hurt. It was better not to respond than to have my daughter hang up on me. I pulled my statistical psychology book over to the counter under the phone. I had a major research paper due and I still had to quantify some of my results. *That* was going to take me a *long* while. I was only half listening to my daughter's soft voice as I flipped through the pages looking for my bookmark.

"You're not listening to me, are you? Are you reading?" Debbie asked, accusingly.

"No. I'm studying — working, really. This is not reading." Not many people, including my daughter, understood my giving up a prestigious management position to go back to school. None of this was easy at my age, competing with the twenty-year old Honors students, most of them wearing Calvin Klein and driving BMWs, at school on full scholarships and full of enough energy to party all weekend when I was *killing myself* trying to learn Algebra at the age of 45.

I slammed the thick blue book shut and grabbed a chair with my foot, dragging it under me, and sat down hard. Maybe I could just talk her through this. I mean, how hard can it be to take care of a five year old? I waited for Debbie to continue her tale of woe. I was mildly irritated about nothing in particular but I thought it might be with the childish whine emanating from my now-grown daughter, reminiscent of days too long ago, and I was wondering how close to the phone this *new to our family* little girl was.

"Mom? Mom, are you there?"

"I'm here, Debbie. What can I do to help?" My hands went up in the air involuntarily, making the Italian sign for, *And so what is it you want from me?*

"You have to come over. Maybe you can talk to Crystal. She needs to eat something, doesn't she? Or do you think they fed her on the plane?"

"I'm sure she needs to eat. It's a long flight from New York." I put my forehead on the countertop, pressing it into the rough hewn wood. This was not going to be a study night. This was obviously a night to train my daughter in the way of five-year-olds.

"Mother! I don't feel good and now I've got this *kid* to take care of!"

"My point exactly, Deb. *You* have this child to take care of and *I* have a report to write." A headache night. I rubbed my temple with my free hand.

My Debbie, barely 20 and pregnant with her first child, learned not too many months ago that her husband had a brief liaison with another woman. The result of that affair had been this now five-year-old little girl. To hear her husband, Rob, explain his side of the story, *he didn't know he had a daughter either until a few months ago,* but he certainly knew at the time he was doing something that might result in such a blessed event. *Surprise, Deb! It's a girl, five years old and she's coming to live with us!*

"I'll be right over, BeeBows," I promised. That slipped out. My third child and second daughter was so not going to like me calling her by an old and happily discarded family nickname. I smiled despite this immediate trauma in Debbie's life, remembering why I called her BeeBows. It came from an old rhyme that I'd made up years before she was born: "She's as cute as a Bow on top of a Bee." Debbie, being one of the world's cutest babies, was always BeeBows to me.

I knelt to say a quick prayer before grabbing my long wool coat from the closet and heading over to their house.

I asked my Heavenly Father for the strength to keep my mouth shut. Besides, I was *furious* that anyone would refuse to replace a baby's misplaced coat. What kind of lesson was that going to teach her? That it's possible to freeze to death in the dead of winter with a foot of snow on the ground in Tacoma, Washington?

Having dusted my knees off, I grabbed my umbrella, slipped into my long coat and pushed the heavy wooden door open against the wind. The snow was already a foot deep and still coming down, the skies making good the promise of a white Christmas. It was December 19th and only six more shopping days to go. I reminded myself to make a Christmas list for Crystal. "Weather unfit for man or beast," came to mind as I pulled plaid wool up over my head and face, leaving just enough space to peek out.

Poor Debbie. The child in my family voted most likely *not* to have any children. The one who never baby-sat, dropped out of Camp Fire Girls, and hated team sports even though she was the best hitter on a little league team called, *The Yellow Bananas, the Team with Appeal.* Debbie had to be dragged to church Primary — not like all the neighborhood children I drove each and every Wednesday afternoon and who couldn't wait to get there.

Debbie had every new baby doll known to little girls as a child — and she never touched them. She was terrified of her Mrs. Beasley doll, and had no use for any baby that wasn't real; needing its pants changed. Instead, Debbie's best friend was our 100 pound boxer, and she forced poor Bumper to sit beside her for hours with a scarf draped over his head while she read storybook after

5

storybook to him. As long as she lived with me Debbie never went Trick or Treating. The whole idea of dressing up, running through the blackest of nights carrying a bag, begging strangers to give you candy, was abhorrent to her. We offered her ice-skating lessons during which I gave her an M & M every time she made the complete circle around the ice-rink. Those lessons lasted one term even though her older sister was a competitive skater and wouldn't get *off* the ice.

Debbie did enjoy her violin lessons and read voraciously. She took violin lessons at school and never sounded like she was *killing the cat*. When I realized how talented she was, I found a teacher away from school. He was known as "Fiddlin' Farley" and taught Debbie how to play country fiddle. She practiced alone in her bright, sunshine yellow bedroom for hours on end. Reading and practicing violin are both activities you can do on your own and that seemed to suit her just fine.

Debbie had the softest, sweetest singing voice but was always too bashful to sing in front of anyone. I could hear my sunshine baby singing church Primary songs in her room and I sometimes stood outside her door, smiling as she sang, "*Jesus loves me this I know . . .*" or "*I looked out the window and what did I see . . .*" I knew she might stop singing if she thought I was listening at her door.

Debbie's big sister Deidra, and her older brother Ronnie, were both married with families. Deidra was the consummate mother and enjoyed her role as parent immensely. Ronnie struggled along but loved his children and was a doting big brother to Debbie. Her siblings and I were amazed when Debbie announced her pregnancy; however; we were not half as surprised as she was.

Now, Debbie was in charge of a strange little girl, probably all twisted with fear and lonely for her family. The last few months had been miserable for Debbie. She'd spent most of the time sick in bed. Debbie still didn't weigh more than 85 pounds and was not much more than five feet tall. With blond hair that curled down to her waist, she looked more like a 13 year old. This new arrangement with the new little girl couldn't possibly work.

Although I had learned to tolerate her husband, he was a drinking man and I had heard him, on more than one occasion, verbally abuse Debbie. I was worried about this new and sudden addition to their family. I didn't think it was fair for my daughter to be taking on this new child when she was expecting one of her own, and it was clearer yet that Debbie didn't need to be dealing with the chaos that was surely going to reign in her home.

As I schussed along the slippery streets toward Deb's house in my just-purchased two-seater sports car, I couldn't help feeling excited to meet my newest granddaughter. I took a detour into the Fred Meyer's parking lot just around the corner from my cabin. I fully intended for that baby to have a warm coat, and Rob could just go jump in the nearest lake if he didn't like it. *Now there's a Christmas thought.*

I bought the little girl a few things to wrap and keep for Santa under my Christmas tree. A *few* things is probably an understatement. Being an expert turbo-shopper, my cart was quickly filled with a bright pink Big Wheel, resplendent with Barbie stickers, one sweet-faced, soft-bodied baby doll, complete with diaper bag and baby bottles, and a few story books. I also found some purple leggings and matching turtleneck shirt, a bright pink hat with a four inch ball of purple yarn on top, and a bag of green and red Hershey Kisses. The quilted, pink and purple snow coat I found sat precariously on top of the Big Wheel, and I had to hold it down as I careened into the check-out line. Waiting in line behind four or five more expert turbo-shoppers gave me enough time to impulsively capture a pink stuffed elephant from it's wire cage and stuff it under my arm. I hoped a size five coat was going to be big enough.

*You shouldn't be buying all this stuff.* Yes. Yes, I should. *Rob is going to be furious.* Who cares? Not me, I argued back and forth with myself. Well, *hooey* on him. If I was the new Nana, then I had buying privileges. Twenty minutes later I was in the lot wheeling and wading through snow drifts to my car.

I knew Debbie wasn't celebrating Christmas and I almost regretted buying the gifts without at least asking her for permission. *I'm sorry, Beebows, but your mother is quite out of control.* Please forgive me, I'd tell her. Not my fault. I was taken over by the Christmas Spirit of Shopping.

"We don't celebrate Christmas," she had carefully explained to me one day early in December.

"You *what*? Of course you do."

"No. Rob doesn't believe in Christmas."

"Debbie, we *always* had a grand Christmas celebration. Family, tree, dinner, presents, Christmas stockings. Why you aren't celebrating Christmas?"

"Christmas is a pagan holiday."

"Oh. Really? Well, that is just ridiculous. Let *him* not celebrate. *You* can come to my house for Christmas." Her husband's religion doesn't celebrate any holidays, but if he didn't practice his religion, why should Debbie? I was trying not to judge his religious practice but I do Christmas, especially if there are children.

I asked my son-in-law, Rob, if I could give Debbie a few gifts for the new baby if I gave them to her the day after the 25th. Debbie had been *quarantined* from me for a month over that discussion.

I never knew what might set her husband off. He had locked Debbie out of the house one afternoon in the snow, and when I threatened to call the police on him, Debbie made up some story about him being asleep and it was her fault because *she'd lost her keys.* My offer to provide my daughter with refuge had thrown me into forced exile for two weeks. I knew buying these gifts would really make him mad, and the few things I bought for their new daughter would have to wait until after Christmas to be given to her, even if she needed them now.

I prayed as I inched through the crowded parking lot, aiming the long nose of my car through softly falling snow toward the 15 minute drive to Debbie and Rob's small, three room apartment. "Heavenly Father? Please soften Rob's heart toward this child and allow her to have this coat. It's so cold this time of year and she'll need to be warm." I hoped He was listening, because it was darn cold. My toes were already numb in my boots and I vowed to get fleece-lined rubber boots for myself. I wondered if the little girl had warm shoes.

The drive took thirty minutes with the combination of heavy traffic and increasingly slick roads. Debbie had sounded so desperate on the phone I could only hope they'd been able to make some progress with the child. Where on earth were they going to put two children and how would they manage financially? I wondered how frightened this child was, having been sent on a plane, clear across the country, to virtual strangers one week before Christmas. I imagined she was terrified and beyond.

"Well, Nana. Here we go," I whispered anxiously, pulling into the visitor's space in front of their tiny, one bedroom apartment. As I parked and got out of my car I hesitated. Should I take the new coat in with me or leave it on the doorstep when I left? It was snowing and the temperature was sure to drop into the single digits by nightfall. The new coat went in with me, along with the pink elephant.

"Mom, meet Crystal. Crystal, this is your Nana."

I waved at the tiny child with one hand as I pulled one glove off with my teeth. "Hi there, Sweetie." I said, wiping snow off my eyelashes.

Then I took a second look at the wee child. Little Crystal was the funniest looking sprite. Not even a yard high, with bone straight, white hair and long bangs that fringed straight out over the biggest pair of crystal blue, almond-shaped eyes I'd ever seen, she stared unblinkingly at me. Her eyes were propped wide open by obvious fear and her bottom lip was pulled over the top of her mouth in a pout.

She was sitting in the corner of their tiny living room on a tattered, brown vinyl recliner, her shoulders up around her ears. Her thin legs barely hit the edge of the chair. This shiny new Crystal was wearing a dark blue, cotton dress with short sleeves. I nearly stopped breathing as I stared breathlessly at this small waif. I recognized her right away and I wondered if Rob or Debbie noticed my inability to move or speak or my heart thumping.

"She looks *terrified*, Debbie," I offered, my words directed at Rob.

"She's not *terrified*. She's mad," Rob interjected.

"Well, what has she got to be mad about?" Rob was such a dolt! Could this baby be angry at being *rejected* by her once custodial grandmother in Connecticut? Maybe being tossed in with complete strangers at the age of five upset her, especially when her "dad" spoke like this:

"Crystal is in big trouble for losing her coat and she has to sit in that corner." Rob loomed a full six feet, one inch tall and was standing with hands on his hips facing his little girl.

"And just how long does she have to sit there, Rob?" I asked through a smile stretched over clenched teeth. I tossed my coat on the sofa, moved passed him, ending up between his imposing figure and my daughter, instinctively trying to shield Debbie and Crystal from his grimace. I could smell the alcohol on him — clearly not a sober man tonight. I knelt down in front of Crystal and she put her toe against my fingers and looked beyond me at her father. She'd never seen him before today, but she knew he was the boss. I didn't take my eyes off the little girl.

"Hi, Sweetie. Are you okay?" My heart was still pounding. I wanted to scoop her up and run from the apartment. I leaned in toward her and she put her forehead on mine. I could feel her baby breath on my face. I was warmed and comforted by her touch. I hoped she could hear my heart beating. I wanted her not to be so afraid.

Before I was pregnant with Debbie I'd had three miscarriages, one right after another. I'd been bedridden for several months. I wanted another child so desperately, but my body just didn't cooperate. When I got pregnant with Debbie, I'd been told I might lose her if I didn't stay completely off my feet for the last several months I was carrying her. I did as I was told and relied on neighbors and friends from church to help me care for my two toddlers. I knew beyond a shadow of doubt that Debbie was a new spirit and the three miscarriages before her were other children, or maybe just one child's deperate attempt to come to me. In any case, I believe I will have a chance to raise them in Heaven.

As this little thing looked up at me I felt such a strong prompting that we'd met before. I heard a strong but silent whisper that tugged at the very marrow of my existence — *This is your child. One that was meant for you.* Then silently I spoke . . . *I know this Angel — I know you, baby. Do you know me?* There were no words — but I thought she might feel what I was feeling, and know me too.

I hadn't ever really pictured the child that I'd been unable to parent, but I had always guessed she was a little blondie, with blue eyes like my baby sister, Wendy. The rest of my children and I have dark complexions with brown eyes. More like my father's Italian side of the family than my mother's Swedish relatives. Crystal looked so remarkably like Debbie did at the same age that they could have been sisters. I was enchanted by the strikingly familiar button nose, slightly long face with fine features, and the same stick-straight white hair Debbie had at the age of five.

Crystal's sweet and gentle spirit reached out and enveloped me. I instinctively opened my arms to her. She flew off the seat and I picked her up, holding her close to my chest. I felt her faintly freckled nose press into my neck. Never mind that it was drippy and her little hands sticky-stuck to my cheeks as she pulled my face around and looked directly into my eyes.

"Who are you?" she demanded to know, her brilliant blue eyes wide, peering straight through to my soul.

"I'm someone that loves you very much."

"Are you sure?" she asked in a surprisingly strong voice. Crystal smiled up at me, a crooked little smile that pushed her top lip out a bit.

I held my breath and closed my eyes, remembering. It was the *same* smile that my younger cousin Susan had bribed us into loving her with years ago. I'd always thought Debbie resembled Susan. And Susan's daughter looks like me. The irony here was that Susan had been adopted by my Aunt LaRee and Uncle Jack. I spent a lot of time with Aunt LaRee as a child and I remember her telling me when Aunt Claire died that when she got to Heaven, she was going to find us a baby girl. It was only a few days after Claire's passing that Susan came to us.

Aunt LaRee and I were both convinced that these sweet spirits are meant for certain mommies, no matter how they arrive. Aunt LaRee used to say, "It's no coincidence that children who are adopted often look just like siblings or cousins. These children are *supposed* to be in your family."

"I'm quite sure I love you," I smiled back at Crystal hugging her tighter. "I've been waiting a long time for you to come see me." I put my nose in her hair and sniffed for the strawberry scented shampoo in which I used to wash Debbie's bleached white-by-the-sun hair every night. I could almost smell . . .

"Well, I'm here now!" she whispered in my ear as she dug herself further into my arms, and deeper yet into my heart.

Debbie and Rob just stood there, staring at Crystal and me holding each other as if we'd been separated for a millennium and then joyfully reunited. I began to cry, weep really, though I felt strangely comforted. Filled with inexplicable joy, I wanted to hold her forever.

"I'm going to call you Chrismiss," I was finally able to choke out.

"Why?" Crystal reached up and wiped the tears off my face.

"Because you are my Christmas Angel."

Crystal reached behind me, pointing at the couch. "Is that my Elfie?" Her smile got bigger and that top lip stuck out straighter.

"I forgot! I did bring you an elephant. A pink one to match your new coat." Putting her down at my feet I held up the cotton candy puff of coat. A size five was plenty big for her. A size three might have been a perfect fit. I slipped her frail arms through the sleeves and hunted for her little hands.

"My daddy said I can't have a coat." Crystal looked up at Rob, her brow furrowing, her sweet smile disappearing. He was silent about the coat, but clearly angry with my breaching his parental authority.

"Ahh. But *Nana* found this coat for you and I'll bet your Daddy doesn't mind you having *this* one. And this Elfie is special too. He's going to stay with you when I can't be here." I wondered how many days I'd have to spend away from Debbie, and now Crystal? Rob stomped out of the room, into the bedroom and slammed the door. Crystal, Debbie and I flinched in unison.

"Chrismiss — Nana is going to have to get you some snow gloves when we find your hands."

"Don't need gloves," she giggled, looking up through her coat sleeves for her fingers.

She did and I was going to get them for her. Debbie went into the bedroom to try and mollify her husband, but not before thanking me for making him mad. I knew that I was making it harder for her, but nothing was going to stop me from welcoming this baby into our family. I knew Debbie wasn't thrilled with her being here. I wasn't sure how Rob felt about his new daughter. And thus began the shortest, hour long visit of my life. Crystal was happy to sit on my lap and ask me how I knew Debbie and Rob, and did I have other kids? Where were they, and why wasn't there a daddy at my house?

With both Rob and Debbie out of the room I got bolder. Not smarter, just more courageous. I chanced bringing the more temporal aspect of the Holiday into the house. "I'll bet Santa Claus will leave some things for you under my tree."

"No. Daddy and Debbie don't have Santa Claus."

"I know. But *Nana* has Santa Claus. I have Christmas at my house. Did you know that's when we have the birthday for Baby Jesus?"

"Is he yoy baby?" Funny. Crystal was very articulate, except she couldn't pronounce her *Rs*. She also didn't know who Baby Jesus was.

"Baby Jesus lived a long time ago and is all grown up. He lives in Heaven and He is someone else who loves you very much. You and I can talk about this some more when you come to my house, okay?" Rob and Debbie came back into the room, just as I was pulling Crystal's new coat off.

"We're tired now, Mom. Crystal, Nana needs to leave," Rob was speaking for Debbie now. They both stood back while I gave Crystal another tight hug.

She can keep the coat, Debbie," I stated more than asked. "And the elephant?"

"Yes, she can keep the coat." Debbie was talking this time. Brave girl, my daughter.

"And the elephant?" Crystal was looking down at her toes again. Shoulders up, and that bottom lip came out again. That wasn't pouting. It was fear. The overpowering stench of fear in this apartment emanated from Rob and permeated every living thing within reach of his voice.

"You can keep the elephant, Crystal," Rob barked. Crystal held the elephant, now known as Elfie, against her chest. Rob and Debbie stood back as I held their new little girl and my sweet granddaughter one last time. I was concerned about her size and even more concerned about her tummy that stuck out too far for such a skinny child. Her hair was brittle and dry. Crystal had all the signs of malnourishment. When I'd helped her put the coat on I'd noticed several dark red marks on the insides of her upper arms. I didn't even have to wonder how they had gotten there.

"Crystal, maybe Debbie will bring you to my cabin this week. It's a lot of fun there. We have kitties in our yard all the time, and squirrels living in our trees." She reached for her coat and stuffed her arms back into the sleeves.

*Christienne Lynae* — that name came to me as I watched her pull the hood of the coat up over her long blond hair. I felt it again — *Christienne Lynae.* Christienne is the female and European spelling of the name Christian, meaning Christ's follower, or the anointed one. I had a *powerful* feeling this child was going to love the Gospel and make every attempt to be Christ-like.

It was obvious to me that Debbie was exhausted and not feeling well. The dark circles under her eyes and gaunt face told a story of sleepless nights, and too much stress. Most of Debbie's stress, I was convinced, was because of her husband, Rob. And the hour was late for a five-year-old to still be up, especially a baby that had just traveled clear across the country. It was all-too-soon time to depart through what was fast becoming a furious snowstorm. After waiting so long to hold this child in my arms, I was loath to leave her.

"Hey, whey-o are you going?" Crystal wanted to know as I stood to get my ankle-length, black coat.

"Back to my cabin, Chrismiss."

"Why don't you live with us?" Crystal scurried down off the chair, put her tiny feet on the toes of my black leather boots and hung onto the fringe of my woolen scarf.

"I'm a big girl and I have my own house, but I'll be sure and come back and see you, okay?" She let go of my scarf to sit on the floor.

"But, when *will* you come back?" she asked, almost plaintively.

"I'm not sure, Honey." I looked up at my daughter.

"Nana will come when she has time. Maybe next week," my daughter answered. So, this latest *infraction* of mine, giving the baby a coat and stuffed toy was going to cost me a week's penance.

When I walked out the door I waved one last time, trying to leave as much love with Crystal as possible, and looking through the window I saw Debbie and Rob going in to their bedroom. I stood and watched that door close and Chrismiss climb back into the corner recliner. *You just hang on to that pink Elfie until I get back, baby.*

*What kind of a Nana leaves a baby by herself!* I was not happy with my daughter either. That *she* would leave this child alone in the living room. *Was Crystal hungry?* I'd forgotten to ask. *Were they going to feed her?* I was crying by the time I got to the parking lot, putting my eyelashes in grave danger of being frozen to my eyelids. My tiny car lunged through the swirling snow toward home, and I could still feel the wee child's breath against my face. I swear I could smell the pleasantly tart scent of strawberries. It was going to be a long night . . .

Leaving the child that I felt I had finally found again was so hard to do. Not that my feeling was even rational. With all my children grown and gone, I'd enrolled in college, finished my AA Degree and then transferred into a private college. The long term goal was to get my BA in Psychology, and I was stumbling through a major in Psychology with a minor in English, supporting my single household by cleaning newly constructed condos at night. The short term goal was to get a decent grade in Statistical Psychology. I was finally without children to interrupt a college study group, and quite frankly, loving not having anyone but me to take care of. My life was about to change *dramatically.*

The first of many emergency phone calls from Debbie came the next morning around 8:00 o'clock. "Mom, Crystal won't eat. She didn't eat dinner last night and she didn't eat breakfast this morning. She wants us to go get her a Burger King hamburger."

"Well, tell Rob to go get her one." Burger King. Two blocks from her house. Surely they could manage that?

"He spanked her and put her in the corner."

"Because she wanted Burger King?"

"No, because she won't eat. He told her she was going to starve herself to death." I could hear Debbie's fear loud and clear. She was in tears. This couldn't be good for the baby she was carrying and certainly wasn't good for Crystal.

"Debbie, listen carefully," I advised, trying to speak slowly and not too harshly. "Children *don't* starve themselves to death. When you were five you wouldn't eat anything but oatmeal with ice-cream on it and french fries from Jack in the Box." *What on Earth was the matter with Debbie? Maybe I should go over once and for all and just punch Rob right in the face!* I was trying to remember that I aced Advanced Logic in college, I was a lady, after all, and I needed to be a good Christian. However; I was also the quintessential Italian mother — like a wild grizzly should harm threaten to befall any of my cubs.

"Can you come over? Mom, please. Just this once."

*Hah! Just this once? No, I can't. Crystal isn't my child.* This is so not my job. Anyway, Rob was going to be furious if he found out how I really felt about Crystal. I wanted to shout, *"Don't ask me to come over, I'm in the middle of a huge project for school. I don't want to get involved. It's still snowing, freezing cold outside, and I'm snuggled in, toasty warm inside my cute little cottage."*

I wanted to tell Debbie all the above and more. I was trying very hard to convince myself not to dash over to their apartment. This could set an inconvenient trend. I was already pulling my coat, gloves and scarf on. I couldn't get in my car fast enough. I rolled through Burger King on the way over to Deb's house. *No child* within arms' length of me was going to go hungry for want of an 99 cent hamburger. Crystal could have it her way, as far as I was concerned. Besides, they were asking — begging for my help. Rob and Debbie didn't want my advice, but they opened this door. I was going to march through it, and it was my *concern* they were going to have to deal with now!

The same bell rang for help each time I left the three of them for more than an hour. Everything was a huge crisis for Rob, Debbie and poor little Crystal. "Mom, she's screaming again, she won't take a bath, she won't eat, she won't fall asleep, she won't let me touch her, I think she hates us. Can you come over?"

I came and went. I drove and left my research project — cleaning — sleep . . . My life was coming unraveled, one thread at a time. I cried on the drive over and cried harder on the way home. It was wrenching to leave the baby in an apartment so filled with unrest, and there was no way I could stay without creating more problems for Debbie. When I had to leave Crystal, I would leave a tiny prayer with her, that Angels would keep watch over her.

Christmas had come and gone without my giving Crystal the rest of the presents I'd bought her, but I kept them wrapped under my two-foot artificial tree, right next to some new clothes I'd wrapped for Debbie. I'd made a few flannel layette items for the new baby and they were wrapped along with Crystal's presents. I had decided to leave my Christmas decorations up until Rob and Debbie agreed to let me bring Crystal home with me to the cabin to visit. So far, that had not been al-lowed, even though I'd asked several times, and been their perpetual rescuer.

I lived in a woodsy, back area of North Tacoma, in a one room cabin with a small loft. The place was perfect for children, lots of land to run and hide in and plenty of children on the block. The long street ending in a cul-de-sac would be a safe place for Crystal to ride her new Big Wheel. I was sure Crystal would love it as much as I did, and even more sure that Debbie and Rob had noticed the bond growing between Crystal and me.

I was at their apartment more than I was at my cabin lately, and I was very grateful to be on break from school. I took treats for Crystal, food for the household that I thought she might like, and a few clothes I'd picked up at the after-Christmas sales. I offered to buy the new baby a crib and was turned down by Rob with a curt, "We don't need any of your help."

Crystal never cried when I left her to go back home, but I new she didn't want to be with them. She never complained to me, instead staying silent while I fed her or read a story to calm her down. As soon as she was quiet I was told by her new parents, *It's time for us to go somewhere,* or *we're tired so you need to leave,* or *we have friends coming over, so come back later.* I'd leave a very dejected Crystal clutching a much needed Elfie, knowing that I'd be called back soon to handle some new crisis. It occurred to me that Crystal was catching on very quickly. If she created *situations,* Nana came running. How long could Crystal and I keep this up before Rob and Debbie caught up with us?

Then finally, exhausted after two weeks of driving back and forth, and Rob being totally irritated with me being in their apartment, the tenuous relationship between Crystal, Rob and Debbie, exploded. I got a phone call from Debbie at 6:00 o'clock one morning shortly after the New Year's weekend. "Mom, Crystal is asking for you again. Can you take her for a few days?"

My poor little Christmas angel was always in trouble for something, and spent most of her waking hours terrified of the spankings Rob was quick to administer. The whole idea of Crystal, the child of Rob's *other woman*, invading her space was wearing thin on my daughter. I was worried about Deb's health, Crystal's well-being and the safety of my unborn grandson.

"What the matter now, Debbie?"

"Mom, just come. Come now. Please." Debbie was crying. Hard. Almost that choking kind of weeping when you can't catch your breath. It frightened me.

"I'll come, Debbie. But you have got to start bringing Crystal to my house once in a while."

"Just . . . come . . . now . . . !" Okay. I'd go. Just this one last time. I wasn't frustrated with Crystal. I knew why she was working this to her benefit and I didn't want her left in their care either. But this was making us all crazy! *Crystal, you and I are going to chat when I get to you.* Then I'd talk to Debbie. Mother to daughter first and then woman to woman. I had work to do and they needed to start being a family — If that was at all possible.

When I got to Debbie's apartment I learned Crystal had again refused to eat breakfast. Rob had picked her up, carried her to the bedroom door and *thrown* her five feet across the room. Crystal's latest flight into terror was broken when her back hit the wooden edge of their water-bed. I was sick just thinking about what he'd done to her — There had to be something I might have done to stop him from going this far. Obviously Debbie was powerless.

When I walked into the bedroom, Crystal was still crumbled over where her tiny body had dropped, at the foot of the bed. Carefully I lifted her up and sat her on my lap. Crystal was not making a sound — silent terror etched on her face, eyes shut tight. My soul tore, rent by pain and guilt for leaving her with my daughter and her husband. I'm so sorry, Angel. I am so sorry. I'm a wretched Nana. This was insane. I had fought it long enough. *I was going to take her with me.* No way was I leaving this house without this child. Where was that monster!

"My — back — hurts, Nana," she whimpered quietly.

"She's not hurt, mom. She isn't even crying, " Debbie justified.

I folded my arms around the scared little bird and rocked her back and forth, nesting her in my arms. I tried not to look at my own child. How *could* she allow this to happen? I'd never even spanked Debbie — *ever.* Not in her whole life.

"How *could* you let him do this to her?" Debbie backed out of the room, terrified herself. I wasn't sure if it was me she was afraid of or of what she thought might happen to *her* when he came.

When I lifted Crystal's shirt up, there was a broad red mark clear across her back that was just beginning to welt up. A mark that was sure to turn into an ugly bruise. Bring her home for just a *few* days? Not on your life!

"Where is Rob?" I asked my now teary-eyed Debbie.

"He's gone. But he'll be back soon, Mom. Can you just take her with you for a little while so I can work this out with Rob?"

"I'll take Crystal home with me, but I want her to stay for more than a few days."

"Just take her and go before Rob gets home. Please." Debbie leaned back into the door, looking like, well, an empty shell. I wanted to gather both of them up in my arms and run back to my cabin. Debbie was practically cowering and it broke my heart. I had to make a decision and that was to protect the child that couldn't protect herself. Debbie was an adult and beyond my help for the moment.

Crystal's clothes were strewn around the room and I grabbed everything I could, stuffing shirts, pants, unders and dirty dresses into the military flight bag Debbie held open for me.

"Debbie, I want you to come with us." Reaching out for her, I wanted to steady her, give her some courage, let her know I loved her and was trying to understand. I had to at least *try* to help my child. I'd seen bruises on Debbie's arms — and asked her about them — but she had always had an excuse for the tell-tale marks. "I can't leave you here alone. We need to call the police."

"I can't, Mommy. He didn't mean it. That's why he left. He felt so badly." There it was. *I was her mommy.* I felt as if I was sacrificing one child to save another. I could call the police, but Debbie would not have signed a complaint against him. Not yet, anyway.

Debbie stood at the door and watched me leave with Crystal under one arm and her bag in the other. But not before I had Debbie sign a paper saying I had their permission to keep her. I was *terrified* of what Debbie might be facing when her husband returned, and I knew she was too. And I prayed as my little car sputtered home in the cold — for us all.

"Are we going to the cabin, Nana?" Crystal looked okay. She still wasn't crying.

25

"Yes, darling. We're going to my cabin."

This child should be ranting, raving, screaming, *something*.

"Does my daddy know how to get there?" She started to whimper, and then a wail escaped from her that all but took the enamel off my teeth. She needed to get it out. This child had been silent for too long, and was afraid her daddy would know how to find her. I began to cry. She began to cry louder. I fumbled around in the glove box for a tape, and popped it in the tape deck.

"Listen to this music, Chrismiss. It's nice. The music will make you feel better." It was a Christmas tape I'd left in the car. I watched her quiet right down — nothing like Bing Crosby's, *Mele Kalikimaka is the Island's way, to say Merry Christmas to you . . ."* to perk us up. We cried all the way to the cabin. And it felt good.

Rob concerned me. I wasn't really clear that he knew I was going to take Crystal home with me, and was pretty worried about what would happen when Crystal's maternal grandmother found out that she was now in another stranger's home. Debbie gave me her number on the temporary paper she'd signed, and I reluctantly made the phone call. Unbelievably, she didn't seem too worried about my having Crystal with me. Especially when I explained how violent Rob had been.

We had one very short, long-distance conversation. She never asked to speak to her granddaughter. I found that odd. I talked to my grandchildren all the time, for longer conversations, asking more questions about what they were up to, and knowing they were safe with good parents. I've made funny noises on the phone to six-month old grandbabies who surely didn't have a clue what I was saying. And I'm absolutely positive that's what grandmothers are supposed to do. However; I had to remember that this grandmother had sent a five-year-old to strangers in the first place. Not only were Rob and Debbie strangers to Crystal — the woman had never even met Rob. She only had her daughter's word that Rob was the biological father.

Unfortunately, the biological *mother* did care that I had Crystal, and she called several days in a row demanding that I return Crystal to Rob and Debbie's custody. Her goal, I suspected all along, had been to handcuff herself to her ex-boyfriend's (Rob's) leather belt. Rob was furious when he got home and found Crystal gone.

He called me demanding I bring her back to his house. We had the same argument on the phone for several days in a row.

"I'm not bringing her back yet."

"Bring her back or we'll call the police and tell them you kidnapped her."

"You do and I'll tell them how you threw this baby across the room! I took pictures of her back and Debbie saw you abuse her."

"Debbie saw nothing. Debbie won't back you up." I had no doubt Debbie would take her husband's side. But I was as forceful as Rob. He wasn't sure what might happen to him if I did turn him in for abusing Crystal. I didn't know it then, but he had an arrest warrant on him for something else he'd done and was just not willing to risk pushing it with me.

I was more than ready to report him to the police,

and I should have. I was hesitant in case the little note Debbie had signed wasn't going to hold up in court. What would become of the child if I were arrested for kidnapping her? They probably would turn her right back over to Rob and Debbie. We were stuck in a perpetual revolving door leading to Building 22. I was caught.

He and Debbie had stopped by a few times, but Crystal still wouldn't talk to either of them, and Rob always ended up stomping out of my cabin with Debbie following meekly behind him. Debbie had the same suspicion I had about the reason for Crystal being sent to them and was happy to disenfranchise herself from both the ex-girlfriend and Crystal. Better she should have kicked her husband to the curb and kept Crystal, but I digress and that really is a different topic. The story of little Crystal slowly bubbled to the surface. Most of the information came from Crystal, and I tried to weed out fact from a five-year-old's version. Away from Rob and Debbie, Crystal was both out-spoken and a brutal truth-teller. Totally unable to pronounce the letter *R*, she would say things like, *Nana, yoy hay-o is a mess today — I wet my bed again 'cause that's what I do — my mommy whey-os hoy undywhey-o to woik,* or *nobody tells me what to do!* Crystal was also able to convince me that she had lived *all ovo the countee!* I knew from Debbie that Crystal had indeed lived all over the country. First with her mother, then the grandmother, back and forth between states and those two for months, then out to California to the maternal grandfather and his new wife, then to the Aunt, back to the mother, a maternal Aunt and Uncle, then back to the grandmother. Crystal had lived with no fewer than five or six family members in her short span on Earth!

After some interesting talks with Crystal, I was able to put some more of the puzzle pieces of her frenetic life together. Crystal's mother was a topless dancer somewhere on the East Coast. It was true my hair was often a mess, especially when it rained, and Crystal cut me no slack on bad hair days. It was also true that she wet the bed every night.

The maternal grandmother actually had custody of both Crystal and her baby sister (whom she was adopting), but no one in their family wanted Crystal. I did find out from the maternal grandmother that her daughter had been drug-addicted to Crystal Methamphetamine when both Crystal and her little sister were born. The father of record (a different man than my son-in-law, the alleged biological father) was currently incarcerated in a state prison. The grandmother wasn't sure whether or not Crystal had been born addicted, but she remembered her daughter had not been allowed to hold the baby because of the drug use.

This baby had been neglected, abused, unwanted, and was clearly malnourished and anemic. The malnourished part I had already guessed by Crystal's brittle hair and round tummy, indicative of children who were deprived of the nourishment provided by a diet of healthy food. The grandmother also told me that she thought Crystal had been *sadly neglected.* The woman was *master* of the obvious.

The grandmother told me she *couldn't handle Crystal* and that her children were mean to Crystal when she lived with them, so the grandmother decided to look up the biological father and send Crystal to him and his new wife, Debbie. For some reason, the trip couldn't wait until *after* Christmas. The maternal grandmother said, "Crystal just can't adjust to family life."

Crystal, whom I began to call Chrissy, thrived when I brought her to the cabin. Not right away, but she was peaceful for longer periods of time. Meal times were a struggle. It was true — she showed no interest in eating. She almost looked afraid of food. But, being Italian, it is imperative that children eat! So we kept trying to find something she liked. Crystal and I stood in front of the pantry forever some days, just looking through the canned goods and moving food from shelf to shelf in hopes that something would sound tasty. We both discovered that she loved Goiled Cheese Samaches. We ate them morning, noon and night. I got tricky and started giving food silly names and it only took a few days before she began to accept other types of home-cooked meals. Gravy was Magic Sauce, broccoli became Forest Trees, waffles were Bumpy Bread, and bananas were Monkey Munches. Chrissy gagged if I mentioned peas or showed her a can with peas on the label.

"My othoy grandma made me eat them. If I thoy up on the floy — she puts me to bed."

"Well then. No more peas for you, Chrismiss." I had no intention of being the reason any child threw up on the floor, or anywhere else.

"Foy whe-als? You gonna promise?" She smiled that funny little way, sticking her top lip out straight.

"For reals. I promise you." It didn't take much to make us happy. No peas at mealtime pretty much did it. I was falling in love with this child. Away from Rob, she became a totally different child. Happy and serene. We adjusted quickly to being together full time. And it was much easier not to be so afraid for her.

We made snow angels every morning, and when the snow melted into an early spring, we took slow walks down to the creek near my house. I cautioned her never to go near any water without me, and we laughed because she never went anywhere without me. Even in the cabin.

"Will I live with you always, Nana?" she asked one day on a walk through the woods in back of the cabin. We stopped to pick up pinecones to paint with peanut butter for the birds.

"I don't know. But we're going to find out soon. I would like that."

"Me too," she admitted, stuffing more pinecones in a plastic bucket.

I knew she wanted to stay. I wanted her to stay. The truth was, I just didn't know how we could make that happen. We hadn't heard from her grandmother for weeks. The mother had stopped harassing us with her daily phone calls and wild demands to give her back to Rob.

I was afraid to rock any boats. Intellectually I knew this arrangement wasn't legal. Emotionally I didn't want to face any day Chrissy couldn't wake up in my house. I don't think I was really ever looking for Chrissy to be my daughter, until I discovered her, and then I realized I'd waited too many years to find her.

Chrissy had never been inoculated, so away to the

Pediatric Clinic we went. She hated anyone strange touching her and had to be strapped down when the nurse took her temperature. She had wax in her ears that had to be scraped out (that wasn't fun for any of us, but she could hear better afterwards) and we got her iron tablets to take for her anemia. The bruises and welts from the spankings Rob dealt her began to heal. The emotional bumps would take years to smooth out, even partially.

One day we were out on a drive, and we stopped at a stoplight. Chrissy unbuckled her seatbelt and slipped down to the floor. "Chrissy, come on. Get back up on your seat."

"Shhhhh, Nana."

"Get up, Chrissy. *Now!* This is too dangerous. I can't drive with you down there."

"No! I can't. *He'll* find me." I looked around. I thought Rob might be following us. I didn't see anyone familiar.

"Who's going to find you?" I tried to reach down to grab some part of her and drag her back up on the seat. Chrissy began to wail and scrunch away, begging me to *hurry past my daddy's house.* We were right in front of some apartments that looked just like Rob and Debbie's.

I pulled over to the side of the road and got her onto her seat again. "No one is going to find you, Chrissy. We aren't anywhere near Rob and Debbie's house." Chrissy huddled against me, shutting her eyes tight. She'd been doing that a lot. It was her way of not seeing the bad stuff. "Open your eyes, Sweetie. So you can see the good things around you." There was so much good in the world, and this little Chrismiss had missed so much of it. If I knew anything, I knew that any good can overpower any bad. We remember the good things longer than bad things, and I was determined that for however long I had Chrissy — she'd have enough good to last her a lifetime.

Chrissy screamed like a banshee when it was time to turn the lights out. She hated the dark (so do I) and I got her a flashlight to keep with her at bedtime. She'd turn that flashlight on and holler, "Okay, Nana. Lights out!" Good idea. Then I got a flashlight for me and wondered why I hadn't thought of that before.

Chrissy refused to get up to go to the bathroom after she was in bed, and screamed if she needed to go, certain I would beat her if the sheets were wet. We devised a game that allowed her to pretend to stay asleep as I carried her to the potty and put her back in bed. No muss, no fuss.

One morning, while trapping dust bunnies in the loft, I discovered she was hoarding food under her bed. I called my psychology professor who advised me that was fairly common in children who had been neglected and who were hungry all the time. He suggested that I talk to her about it and ask if she wanted to keep some snacks with her all the time. Chrissy did not mince words — she told me her mother would forget to feed her, and she would get up late at night and sneak the roommate's food, for which she was hit. That's her word . . . hit . . . "They *hit* me," Chrissy said quietly but emphatically. For eating food.

"We have lots of food here. Why do you keep food under your bed, Chrismiss?" I had no doubt she'd tell me.

"So I have it when I get hungry again." Not if —

*when* she got hungry again. She had learned to be hungry unless she was taken to the nightclub by her mother and the club owner gave her food.

"You don't need to hide food here. Nana has plenty of food for you." But, nothing convinced her that mealtime was going to be a regular occurrence. Why should she believe me? All she'd ever known was hunger. When Chrissy felt the need to stash food under her bed, we zipped it in baggies so we didn't get bugs. She had a Mickey Mouse suitcase filled with Ritz Crackers, Chinese Rice Snacks, apples, dried apricots and goldfish crackers. It took three months for her to feel safe enough with me to sleep all night and to trust that meal times were a regular event at my house. She finally stopped asking at every mealtime, "Is this really my food?"

Chrissy followed me everywhere I went in the cabin. It was a small place, one room on the ground floor and half a loft upstairs, and she could see me no matter where I sat, stood or tried to take a nap. If I stood up, Chrissy stood up with me, grabbed my shirt, hung on with both hands and walked with me. Despite her unwillingness to be touched by anyone else, she never let go of me. I didn't see the inside of the bathroom alone for weeks.

"Chrismiss? Can you just give me a moment?" I'd plead, trying to shut the door without letting her in.

"Nana, I don't have any moments," she'd say with her most serious face. She didn't really. Chrissy had been left alone far too many times to trust me behind a closed door.

We sang *My Funny Valentine* to each other on February 14th and taped leprechauns all over the windows of the cabin on Saint Patrick's Day. On Easter weekend we colored 10 dozen eggs and hid them all over the yard, and then invited my two grandchildren over, along with twenty or so of the neighborhood children, for an egg hunt. My granddaughter, Ashley, and Chrissy were just about the same age, and were becoming fast friends.

I suspected she might have a problem focusing on given or specific tasks. She had trouble holding a pencil and subsequently had trouble forming letters or numbers. Drawing and coloring in books were her least favorite things to do. I thought she might be slightly behind developmentally. I couldn't have been more wrong about that. Chrissy was way ahead of her time in street smarts and common sense. Her lack of fine motor skills was probably due to the biological mother's drug use during pregnancy. The distrust and lack of basic skills — bathing, brushing teeth and knowing there was broccoli in the world was certainly due to the mother's non-existent parenting. *Healthy environment* was an oxymoron in Chrissy's world. Chrissy had a slight speech impediment — just couldn't say her *Rs* — so we practiced those daily.

"Can you say, *girl*, Chrissy?"

"Yes, I can. Goil!"

"Okay, try *floorrrrrrr*."

"Floyyyyyy . . . See? I can do it!" She thought she was saying it right! I sat in front of her with my mouth in a puckered *rrrrrrrr* shape. I must have looked like an idiot to her. I called my psychology professor again to talk to him about Chrissy's speech problem.

"Jerilyn, you have a ton of problems with this child, and it's not her *Rs*." Give the man an A+. He was right.

I didn't stop working with Chrissy on her *Rs*, but I did stop worrying about the way she spoke and instead started enjoying more the words she said. Chrissy was adorably bright and had a bouncy way of speaking. She loved to sing, dance, spin, hop, jump, and run. There were no sleep credits for Chrissy. The faster she went — the faster and longer she could go. She was also extremely logical. I like that in a baby. Chrissy had better reasoning skills than most of the adults I met.

And then . . . there were days that I understood Chrissy's grandmother not being able to keep her. Especially since she had three boys of her own and was taking care of the baby sister. Chrissy had days that she just couldn't get a grip on anything logical, and once she got going, there was no way to pull her back. "I want orange juice!" she would decide.

"We don't have any orange juice. We have apple juice." Chrissy's eyes got as big as dinner plates and wild. Red sky. Monsoon coming. Batten down the hatches and head for the cove.

"I need orange juice! *Give me some!*" Down to the floor she'd go, kicking and screaming.

"You can have juice but it's going to have to be apple." I knew we were sailing into a tempest, and if we didn't get sucked into the Chrissy whirlpool, we certainly capsized, and it took a while to right our ship. Her unexplained storms blew in from nowhere and ended just as suddenly. We didn't have to head for cover every day, or even every week, but she churned our smooth seas into a tidal wave for hours, forcing us through gales of tears and screams that left us exhausted and totally unable to figure out how all that emotion could come from such a tiny child, or why.

"Why do you scream like that, Chrismiss?" Chrissy sprawled across my lap hiccuping and sniveling.

"I . . . *hic* . . . don't . . . *hic* . . . know . . . *hic*." Later she found her way back into my arms. "I am so sowwy, Nana. I don't mean to. I even love apple juice." And then she would sit with me for an hour or so, whispering, "I'm sowwy."

"It's okay, Chrissy. We're quiet now."

"But I am so sowwy."

"Shhhh, Angel. It's all over." I'd brush her sweaty bangs back and kiss her forehead.

"We're fine and we're going to listen to music now."

"Are you mad, Nana?" How could I be? What did she think? That I'd send her away because she'd thrown a fit? I hadn't begun to hear half of what this child had been through, nor could I understand being *thrown away* like an old babydoll. How long does it take to forget that kind of emptiness?

Singing or listening to music seemed to calm Chrissy down, and boy did we sing.

We sang songs that we knew and when we ran out of those we made songs up. Chrissy was happiest when she sang. Her voice was tiny but she sang perfectly on key, even without the music. Once in Pic & Sav, a woman in the check-out line tried to give her a dollar after she sang *JESUS LOVES ME*. I taught her all the Sunday School songs I sang with my kids and she laughed and clapped when I forgot the words. I hadn't been going to church regularly, but I knew that going to church with Chrissy would be a good thing.

Chrissy had an engaging smile and an infectious laugh. It was impossible for her to stand still when she got the least bit excited. My friend Sherry and her daughter were our best friends, and she tended Chrissy for me when I had something at school. They formed a fast bond and I appreciated having someone to help care for my new charge. Sherry liked that Chrissy was so excited about everything good and Chrissy was filled with joy and loved to share news of our life at the cabin with Sherry and her daughter, Heather. Sherry was the one respite I had from my *Velcro baby*. I thought we might find some new playmates for Chrissy at church.

Chrissy and I found a chapel close to the cabin and started to attend church on Sunday. This was, for the most part, a huge nightmare. She hated to leave my side, but I wanted her to learn I was coming back to get her after class and that she was safe in Heavenly Father's house. I never made it through a class without the Primary people coming to get me. Chrissy spent the whole class-time bouncing, crying, turning chairs over and pulling her dress clean over the top of her head.

It was the same problem I had with her anywhere. She was so fearful of crowds, I never knew when something would frighten her and off she'd go, running through the store. Strangers and loud noises sent her screaming down hallways and out the door. A balloon popping resulted in Chrissy slapping her hands over her ears and cowering in the corner. I started using a baby's wrist leash to tie her to me in public places. And then I'd pray there wouldn't be any popping balloons, backfiring cars or big crowds to surge through.

At one time I thought it might be best to just not go out at all. Chrissy and I would simply stay at the cabin where we would both become crazy hermits with long unkempt hair and long yellowed nails. We could forage for food in the back woods, live on earthworms and squirrel stew.

One Sunday, when I was called again to come save her Primary teacher from certain insanity, I found Chrissy lying in the hallway outside her Sunday School classroom. She was moaning and rolling around trying to kick the walls with her new patent leather, Mary Janes. I tried to pick her up and took a toe to the forehead, so I did what any reasonable adult would do. I sat on the floor next to her and began to cry. I reached out again to pick her up and she planted those cute little feet right across my chest. I grabbed her and fell on top of her to stop her from kicking and rolling.

"Oh my. Is that your new little girl, Jerilyn?" I looked up through a ten-inch long piece of my hair, escaped from what used to be a neat little bun on top of my head, directly into the sweet face of a woman I greatly admired, the wife of one of our church leaders.

"Uh, yes. This is Chrissy."

"She is beautiful isn't she? What a pretty dress you're wearing, Chrissy," she complimented. "I've prayed so for a little girl. How lucky you are. I've got five rough-housing little boys, you know. I love them all, but it would be so fun to have a little girl."

Well . . . *there* was another perspective. And I have to say that her kind and thoughtful words changed the Sunday experience for both of us. I got firmer with Chrissy, then bribed her teachers with homemade rolls and into agreeing not to call me out of class anymore. Chrissy learned to stay put, and I learned to put shorts on her under dresses.

Chrissy began to feel safer, and the infrequent visits from Rob and Debbie stopped all together. Again, I felt like I was losing one child to take care of another. Debbie and I had always had a special relationship. She was my baby. My golden girl with the sweet, soft countenance. I missed her, but relieved Rob wasn't bothering us.

Classes started again for me and I enrolled Chrissy in a year round Kindergarten. After her short day she attended a day-care center at my school and we ate lunch sometimes in the cafeteria on campus or I picked her up and dropped her at Sherry's.

I gave up my night job at Chrissy's request. "Nana, you woik *too* much. I want you to stop." Done. No point in having a little girl that spent the whole of her life alone or with strangers and then leaving her alone with more strangers.

"I won't leave you at night anymore unless I have to." One almond shaped eye squinted in my direction. Chrissy didn't believe me. I wanted more than *anything* for this little girl to trust me. I had offers from friends at church to watch Chrissy while I cleaned apartments but I knew in my heart it wasn't right to leave her, not on a regular basis.

I stopped working at night and started editing and typing college papers and resumes at home to earn extra money. My life and Chrissy's, although not routine, settled into something quite regular. She could at least count on the Minerva brand of normal, and I couldn't imagine a time that I hadn't had Chrissy with me. The absence of Debbie left a hole in my heart that even Chrissy couldn't fill, but she came really close.

It became more and more obvious to me that Chrissy, although chased by devils some days, was a smart little gal. She had a great ability to *figure things out.* "That box will fit in the hole, Nana. You just need to lift up one side." Or, "Even if we plant those strawberries today — this minute — we won't have them for breakfast tomorrow, but we will before I turn five, and that's okay because I can wait." She was right. Chrissy knew how long things took to grow, and was incredibly patient...about some things.

Chrissy had also grasped some very basic Gospel principles. On the way home from church one day I asked the requisite question, "What did you learn at church today?"

"I learned at church, that the nicer you are to people, the nicer they'll be to you." Unfortunately this was one child who had some very different experiences in her short life. "But that's not true, is it?" she asked, with her *I'm looking for information face* — one eye almost shut, head down, the other wide open, questioning.

"Most of the time it is, Chrismiss. Some people are very nice."

"But not always?" Chrissy looked so sad. Disappointed, really. So many adults had let her down. She knew how it felt to be so hungry it was safer to save food rather than eat it all in one sitting. Chrissy knew that sometimes the people who are supposed to love you the most, want you the least. And she knew that sometimes, as good as you tried to be, it wasn't enough for someone called *Daddy* to stop throwing you around or hitting you.

I wasn't sure I could protect her or for how long I would be able to keep her. I only knew that I was going to try and . . . well, I could try and adopt her. I didn't know if it would be possible, but I had to at least look into that possibility. I wanted her with all my heart. I didn't want to be another person in her life that didn't hang on to her. Chrissy was special and I had no intention of hurting her. Or letting her go without making an honest attempt to keep her safe.

One day while I was typing a resume for a client, I felt Chrissy standing behind me. "Can you give me a moment to finish this work, Chrissy? Then we'll have a story."

"I have some moments, Nana. But I think you should know where the writing goes when you turn off your computoy."

I stopped typing to pull Chrissy up on my lap before I asked, "Where does it go?" I wasn't sure I had that concept nailed down.

"It goes way inside to a special place, and when you need it the computoy thinks about it and finds it foy you. Just like inside my head. At night the lights go out and I fall asleep. When I wake up I know just how to find things." That was it. Chrissy was like a book called *Life for Dummies.*

We moved from the beginning of Spring to the beginning of Summer. I was done with school for the year and Chrissy and I planted flowers and watched the rain water them in the afternoons. We signed Chrissy up for the school track team and they signed me up to be the Team Mother. Chrissy was fast as a bullet. Who knew she could run that fast, jump that high, throw the ball that far? The coach loved her, and Chrissy hated going. She wanted to run up and down our street so her desire to run wasn't the problem. It took us a while to figure out Chrissy hated hearing the starting gun go off. As usual, she hadn't complained, just didn't want to go. Chrissy wasn't a girl you could *make* do anything. I liked that about her.

It wasn't long before they discovered her singing voice at school. "Nana — guess who gets to be the Puppy in the school play?"

"Hmmmm. Your best friend?"

"No! Guess again."

"Your teacher?"

Chrissy jumped up and down clapping her arms. "It's me, me, me! And I get to sing, too!!" She flew at me, almost knocking me down. "I love you so, Nana. I want to sing *always!*" Well, she knew what she wanted to do with the rest of her life, and I wasn't sure what tomorrow was going to bring. We borrowed a video recorder from Sherry and taped the Puppy play. It was so fun watching Chrissy with her friends. She didn't have just one special friend — she gathered up children in a group and loved them all. She was happy when her people were happy and cried with them when they were sad. Her teacher loved her, and so did her classmates. Chrissy got an award at school for being the friendliest child in the classroom.

She stopped hoarding food, finally trusting me to feed

her — sometimes cheese sandwiches, and sometimes Burger King on a busy day, but we had three hots and a cot and she could count on that at least. We both slept like we were in comas at night — all night long, and the batteries in our flashlights didn't get used up as quickly. I was finally able to go into the bathroom without her and actually shut the door without having to shove her back with my foot. We adopted a cat that she immediately called, Vestoy.

"Why do you call the cat, Vestoy?" I asked her the first week we had him. He was a great kitty, a fat silver and black Tabby.

"Not that name, Nana. His name is *Vestoy!*" She gave me one of those, *You can't be that stupid* looks.

"Okay. I got that part, Chrissy. But — where did you learn that name?"

"Off the television. You know. Vestoy and Tweetie Bird."

"Chrissy — you mean Sylvester and Tweetie Bird."

"Right. Vestoy and Tweetie Bird."

I got it now. All in the communication. "The kitty is Vester, short for Sylvester?"

"Nana, yes! Like Chrissy is shoyt for Chrismiss." I hoped she'd forgotten her real name was Crystal. I didn't want her to loose her *identity,* but I did want her to forget her past.

Vester and Chrissy were inseparable. Chrissy took total responsibility for him, feeding him, brushing him (which he allowed for hours on end), and reminding me daily to clean out his litter box. "Would you like our littoy box to be doity?" she'd point out to me if I forgot. The cat slept across her legs every night and sat on her desk when she drew pictures or worked on her school papers. Vester came to Chrissy like a well-trained dog when she called for him, and he wagged his tail when she ran to get his grooming brush. Life was good. For all of us.

Then, the last week in June, I got a phone call from the East Coast grandmother. "I want Crystal back. I'm sending you an airline ticket." My knees buckled and I folded myself into the end of the couch. This couldn't be happening. How could I let this baby go back? Six months they left her here with me and now they want her back? And yet, she wasn't mine. Not legally. I thought how easy it would have been to pack us both and head for the border. I wondered how I could have been stupid enough to get so attached to this child. I had to let her go.

I couldn't find the words to tell Chrissy. She knew something was wrong. Terribly wrong. I tried to find a way to tell her, but with a few days left I was praying for a miracle.

Her blue eyes wide with the same fear I'd seen the first time I met her, she summoned up the courage that had deserted me and asked quietly, "Nana? What's wrong with us? Do we need to listen to music?" *She* was trying to calm *my* spirit with song. With only two days left before her flight, I tearfully began to pack her clothes and toys while she slept.

I still hadn't told her she was leaving. "Chrissy, come here to me," I solemnly directed her to do. She didn't move toward me like she normally did. She didn't want to know, whatever it was, anymore than I wanted to tell her. When I told Chrissy what was going to happen — that her Grandmother wanted her back — she stopped talking. Chrissy never said another word. I wanted to hear her sweet voice reminding me to do my chores. I wanted to hear her sing. To *scream* for orange juice when all I had was apple. My heart shattered like a thin pane of glass in a winter storm while Chrissy shut her heart behind a steel door, slammed tight against the horror of a reality she had tried so hard to forget.

Her silence was unbearable for both of us. I could barely stand to look at her. Chrissy sat still and silent on the stairway, staring straight ahead, biting her nails until they bled. I want to believe I was prompted by my Heavenly Father to write my name and phone number in everything she owned. Looking back, it was my absolute terror that this child would not be cared for and the prayerful hope that someone might find my name and phone number and get her back to me. The insides of her shoes, all her books, her toys and baby doll bottoms, the backs of unders, and the tags of dresses were now permanently marked with my monogram. The morning she was to leave I hung a crystal heart suspended on a silver chain around her neck. It had been a Mother's Day gift from my children, Deidra, Ronnie and Debbie. I'd had it for years, tucked away in the bottom of my jewelry box. Etched across the front was a single word — LOVE. I could only hope that I'd had Chrissy long enough to help her understand what love felt like. "Don't take this off, darling," I whispered. "Wherever you are, Chrismiss, you'll know how much we love each other and that I'm always in your heart. You'll always be in my heart, too. Do you understand that?" Still silent, she climbed into my lap, buried her nose in my neck and fell asleep for the last hour we had together.

I drove Chrissy to the airport, and parked as far from the terminal as I could. I wanted to walk, holding her hand, one last time. Chrissy held my hand but still refused to look at me. I can only imagine what she was thinking. *One more person who won't keep me.* How could she ever trust me again? Or anyone for that matter? I walked with her down the gangway, and buckled her into her seat. Chrissy immediately began to scream, and grabbed two hands full of my long blond hair. The flight attendants thought it best I leave. Chrissy's shrieks of raw terror felt like a thousand pieces of shrapnel hitting my body.

"I love you, Chrismiss. More than *anything*. I don't want you to leave, but you have to go back to your Grandmother, because she loves you."

"Noooooooooo! Don't leave me here!" Finally, she'd found her voice. I was asked again to leave the plane and when it became apparent to the attendants I was unwilling to leave her, they held me by both arms and I was escorted back down the long narrow gangway.

I watched, sobbing through the plate glass windows, until the plane taxied down the runway, took flight, and left Chrissy and me alone. Miserably alone. I don't remember leaving the airport, and barely remember the drive back to the cabin. I went to bed for a week and sobbed uncontrollably for most of that time. I didn't answer the phone and I refused to let anyone in the cabin, even Sherry.

Agonizing over every moment I'd felt frustrated or

snapped at Chrissy, I wanted to find her and fix all the times she might have felt lonely with me. I wished I'd let her stay with me in my Sunday School classes. I hoped she knew how much I loved her and understood I hadn't wanted to send her back. I thought again, maybe I should have just left town with Chrissy, taking us both away from anyone who might think of separating me from a child that I knew had picked me to be her mother. And I prayed for us both, and that she would be kept safe. July passed, along with Chrissy's sixth birthday. I sent presents to the grandmother's house but I didn't hear from them. I called and left messages that garnered no response. I was out of Chrissy's life, and obsessed with the thought that she might be afraid, lonely or hungry. I knew that the maternal grandmother had legal custody of Chrissy, but I was pretty sure Chrissy had been returned to her abusive mother. Even though I was able to pull myself out of the abyss left by the absent Chrissy, the pain of losing her never lessened. The thought of Chrissy's huge blue eyes, finally bright with happiness, and her sticky hands holding my face close to hers was tattooed across my heart.

At night, when the cabin was quiet and dark, the clanging memory was deafening as I remembered the look of pain in her eyes when I untangled her fingers out of my hair and left her writhing against the seat belt on the plane. Just thinking about that day could stop my heart. I never knew when that wave of despair was going to wash over me. I was afraid for both Chrissy and me. Eventually, I settled into a quiet hopelessness and crawled slowly through the days one at a time. I sang to her all the time — a song by Kenny Loggins — a song I hoped she could hear in her heart.

"*. . . Though you grow away, No matter how you change, I'll know you. When you tire of life alone, there'll always be one sure way back home. Just turn on the quiet, close your eyes, and listen inside, unconditional, unconditional, unconditional. I'll be there to sing to you, I promise you, I promise to comfort you . . .*"

I sang and cried — the song tormenting instead of calming me. Tried to forget her sweet strawberry smell and couldn't — stayed busy enough to make it through most days. Staying in the cabin without Chrissy was inconceivable. I drove to Utah to visit my daughter, Deidra and her husband Jeff, hoping that being with my four grandchildren would ease the pain of losing Chrissy. It did help, but loving my grandchildren confirmed for me just how much Chrissy was supposed to have been with me.

After I returned to Tacoma in August, the decision not to stay at the cabin was easier for me to make. Convinced that I needed to be closer to my family, I decided to leave Washington state, and move back to San Diego. Debbie and Rob had already decided to move to Arizona. Rob had forbidden Debbie to see me, and I hadn't been allowed to see their new baby boy. I had dropped a few baby things off on their front porch months before and hadn't heard from them since.

Before I left for California, I called the maternal grandmother and told her I was moving, and left my sister's phone number with her, *just in case.* She didn't offer any news of Chrissy, except to tell me everything was fine and I should stay out of their lives. I wondered if Chrissy had gotten my presents and if she missed me.

The move back to San Diego was easier than I thought. I didn't miss anything about Washington, except the months I had spent in the cabin with Chrissy. I was just settling into a new home in San Diego, a new job, and was beginning to pull myself out of the angst due to the loss of both my girls. I had justified my loss by convincing myself that Chrissy had a right to be with her biological family. She needed to be close to her baby sister. All those things had to be good for Chrissy. It was a way for me to survive the loss and go on.

Then, eight days before Christmas, and six months after the nightmare at SeaTac Airport near Tacoma, I got a phone call from Chrissy's grandmother on the East Coast. "Hi, Jerilyn? I just got Crystal back from her mother. I can't keep her. If you send me a ticket, I'll give her to you." Could it really be this simple? I'll *give* her to you? There are people who just give little girls away, take them back and then *return* them?

There was a social worker in the house and the grandmother put her on the phone. It was made clear that if I didn't take Chrissy back she would be placed in a foster home, forthwith. I listened to the social worker explain that the grandmother, against a court order, had indeed returned Chrissy to the biological mother. Chrissy had been beaten and *nearly starved to death*. A day-care provider called the police when she discovered bruises on Chrissy. Chrissy had also been left in her care for several days at a time, without additional clothing or money for food.

My worst fears had been confirmed. Chrissy's grandmother hadn't wanted her after all. I believed then she gave Chrissy back to her biological mother in order to keep Chrissy's baby sister. Kind of, give me the baby and I'll give Chrissy back to you. The grandmother had deliberately delivered Chrissy back into the arms of Evil in order to keep Chrissy's little sister. Chrissy's day-care provider found my phone number in some of Chrissy's clothes and gave it to the police who contacted the grandmother. If I hadn't called back east and left my phone number when I moved to San Diego, they wouldn't have been able to find me.

The social worker told me that Chrissy kept repeating, "I want to go live with my Nana in Washington." That was me! I was crying and jumping around the room. I didn't want to appear too excited, or not excited enough, too maternal or not maternal enough. I agreed to take Chrissy, but only if the Department of Social Services on the East Coast would allow for paperwork giving me temporary custody with the intent to adopt.

I couldn't even be outraged that Chrissy's grandmother didn't want her despite adopting Chrissy's baby sister. It worked for me, and all it was going to take was an airline ticket to get my Chrismiss back. Social Services faxed me the paperwork giving me temporary custody and I prepared to bring Chrissy home. I spent the rest of the day on my knees, thanking Heavenly Father and asking . . . okay, *begging* him for the strength to care for this broken little bird again.

I Federal Expressed a plane ticket back East the next morning. I was a wreck waiting for Chrissy to fly back to me. I called the airlines over and over again to make sure the flight was on time. My sister, Wendy, and I drove the twenty miles to the airport in plenty of time, but inside I was informed the plane was in early and everyone had deplaned. Once again, Chrissy was alone and probably scared, thinking that I wasn't there for her.

"I'm going to run, Wendy. I've got to find her. Meet us at baggage claim!" I took off running down the long halls to the gate.

I ran and ran . . . right past the gate . . . and then I heard a small, familiar voice yell, "Nana! Hey! They-o goes my Nana!"

I stopped and turned around, looking for her. She stood against a wall, holding the hand of an airline attendant. Chrissy was wearing a cream-colored blouse over a skirt that hung two sizes too big for her. She flopped toward me, wearing shoes at least two sizes too big. I almost didn't recognize her. The mother, in her latest drug-induced rage, had chopped Chrissy's long hair off, in some places to the scalp. No matter. The hair would grow. Chrissy was six months older and still the size of a tiny three year old.

This was one plucky little girl who knew what she wanted and wasn't afraid . . . of anything. She flew 3,000 miles by herself again to make it happen. When I knelt down to pick her up, she whispered, "Yoy my mommy now. I'm not going back."

"You don't have to, Chrismiss."

"Foy whe-als?"

"For reals." I felt her nestle into my arms, then a runny little button nose pressed into my neck. Two tiny little hands reached out and stuck quickly to my cheeks. I finally freed myself long enough to look through a flood of tears into her huge, crystal blue eyes, fringed with brown lashes. It was December 19th, exactly one year to the day from the moment I'd first found my Chrismiss.

We stopped on the way home and bought Chrissy some new black, patent leather shoes and got an ice-cream. She hugged her new Auntie and held her new baby cousin, Alexander's, hand all the way home. Even with the few moments of smooth sailing we enjoyed on the trip home from the airport, it was going to take Chrissy months to recover after being with her biological mother.

We'd lost some emotional ground, and climbing back up that mountain, I imagined, was going to be quite a hike. I didn't care then because, even though I'm a realist, I can sure get lost in the ideal. I tend to move ahead wearing blinders and sometimes that's not entirely a bad thing. Chrissy and I had been through a trial by fire, but Heavenly Father was letting us know that we could survive, and our lives would somehow be better for it. Forged of the same steel that protected Chrissy while she was away, our love would help us endure.

Later that night, when I was rocking my sweet child to sleep, she snuggled in close to me and put her hands on my face. "Mommy, will Santa know whay-o I live now?" "Indeed, he will. And we're going to get the fattest tree we can find. Then we'll get a big red stocking and put your name on it. Santa will find you for sure."

Her eyes lit up and I marveled at the resilience of God's children. I'd found Elfie, Chrissy's puffy pink elephant in the closet when I'd moved out of the cabin. I'd almost given it away, several times. Now I could stick it under the tree for Chrissy.

"Do you *promise?*" She looked straight into my eyes, right into my soul and waited for my answer. I knew then, somehow, Chrissy trusted me again. And now I trusted in miracles again. Especially miracles that come at Christmas.

"Yes, I do. I *promise* you." And Chrismiss, you are still my Christmas Angel."

# EPILOGUE

Chrissy and I got through the Holidays, staying busy going to see Santa, visiting some of the attractions in San Diego, like the Zoo and Seaport Village. Chrissy loved everything and within a few days was charming everyone, including her new mommy with that same infectious laugh. We visited the zoo animals, the children's train in Balboa Park and the clowns and carousel down by the water. We popped corn to string on the Christmas tree and visited with family. And this time Chrissy got to open her presents on Christmas morning. Santa found her on Christmas Eve, and next to her beloved Elfie stood a new bike with training wheels. Chrissy hadn't lost her ability to share and spread joy generously. The bike sent her into such a state of happiness we couldn't help but travel there with her. The first time she rode down the driveway, wobbling first to the left and then back to the right, we were all clapping, laughing and jumping up and down. One of our favorite family adages is, *Only happy, smiling people allowed here.* Chrissy fit into our family just fine.

We still ate food with silly names, but this time Chrissy didn't need to hide food packed into baggies under her bed. The first time my sister, Wendy, heard Chrissy ask if the food on her plate was really hers, she had to leave the room, tears flowing down her face. It was as hard for Wendy as it had been for me to imagine any child being so hungry that they needed to hide food, saving it in case there wasn't going to be food to eat later.

Chrissy asked because she just needed to be *sure*.

Our days were much easier than evenings. Chrissy began to have nightmares that terrified us all, and most nights I rocked her to sleep. She woke up screaming every time I tried to put her down. When I had rocked myself out of patience, then Wendy took over and rocked Chrissy. Some nights we brought Baby Alex in and all four of us slept in a double bed. This time it didn't scare me — I knew it would pass. And it did. Within a few months Chrissy was able to lie down in bed with her flashlight and fall asleep, Elfie and our cat, Vester, happy to take the night duty.

As Chrissy got older, it was more evident there were some residual problems from the birth mother's choice of drugs, Crystal Methamphetamine. Chrissy's fine motor skills were lacking and she still couldn't tie her shoelaces. She had trouble holding a pencil, writing her letters or numbers, and couldn't spell her name. I decided to home-school her until we could catch up. As the days passed, her inability to sit still for more than thirty seconds was exhausting us. She still hung on to me and followed me everywhere I went. This time the bathroom was off limits as a joint venture so she sat outside the door waiting for me. As soon as Chrissy began to trust that I wouldn't send her back to her biological mother, she began to trust that when I walked away from her, I would come back. Day by day we deposited small amounts of love and security into a *trust* account. When Chrissy questioned her place in the family, it was only because she just needed to know that I would never deliberately stay away from her.

Deidra and Jeff moved back to San Diego with my

four beautiful grandchildren and were a tremendous support system for Chrissy and me. We moved into the same school district, and Chrissy was able to go to school with her new cousins until she got used to the idea of being away from me for several hours at a time.

All things grow with love, and so did we. Despite a diagnosis of ADHD, Chrissy has learned to focus on tasks at hand and is just raucous enough to let me know that God isn't finished with her yet. She's an exemplary student, extraordinary athlete (having broken her own school record for the mile run four years in a row at the Jr. Olympics) and has installed four Presidential Awards in her Book of Remembrance. We home-school now and are really enjoying that time together.

Chrissy still has a beautiful singing voice — stronger now, and she loves to sing solos at church or for family gatherings. She loves to act, dance, flip, spin and jump, but mostly she loves to share the music in her heart by singing. Although, Chrisy's real talent lies in her ability to feel what other feel, whether that be joy or sorrow. Her empathy for others and her willingness to serve is always evident, and I am in awe of her love for her brothers and sisters, and her love for our friends.

Chrissy and I have hoed some long rows together. It hasn't been easy, but as Chrissy is fond of saying, "We are so lucky to be together." After years of sharing lots of love, learning new skills, and picking bushels of patience, Chrissy is now one of the most genuinely happy children I have ever met. She bounces through life, wakes up singing, rushing to embellish anyone in the house with hugs and morning kisses.

Chrissy asked me one day, why she had to be born to her biological mother instead of coming straight to me. She wondered that if God loved her so much, why did he let her suffer for so long? I explained that I'd had surgery after Debbie was born and was unable to have more children. I told her that she had to get to Earth somehow, and I tell Chrissy again and again what my Aunt LaRee told me when I first got her, that *there's more than one way to get to Chicago.*

After years of trying to cajole Chrissy's biological grandmother to sign our adoption papers or at least produce the paper work that proved the biological mother had been stripped of her parental rights, I filed Guardianship papers. The biological mother and grandmother retaliated by suing me for custody. I was terrified I might lose Chrissy again. I had to gather my strength, pray, and then fight like heck. No way were these people going to snatch this child away from me again. Both courts, one on the West Coast and the other on the East Coast, decided in my favor.

Chrissy and I have once again traveled a long and winding road that healed us both, toward the completion of a journey that will bind us together for this lifetime and beyond. The path has been wrought with pits and bumps, but we haven't hit any signs that say Not A Through Street. We've had days we were convinced we weren't going to make it and days that we are more than satisfied that families really are forever. I don't ask too many questions about how or why I found this delightful child, because: For many of life's trials there are no answers, and God does not owe us any. It is up to us to gave faith that somehow, everything is in his plan.

A few Christmases ago, I took custody of three more grandchildren. A boy two years older, a medically fragile baby, and a little girl four months younger than Chrissy. Chrissy welcomed everyone with open arms, sharing all she had willingly, including a mommy she'd had all to herself for several years. Chrissy has two of the qualities I wish we all had — empathy and an integrity that belies her age. She knows what it is to hurt, and she had learned what love feels like. Chrissy made it possible for me to care for all our new children by helping me to love them. She used to tell the new little waifs, "You'll like it here. There's lots of love in this house."

Chrissy was 12 years old on July 12th of 2000. Her Golden Birthday. She is growing into a beautiful young woman, my Chrismiss. And I believe with all my heart it was Chrissy that so many years ago made such a valiant attempt to become a part of me. I also believe she *chose* to make so many sacrifices the first five years of her life in order to find her way into my family. What a strong spirit Chrissy has. Each time I look at her I remember how truly unique she is and I always have the feeling I'm looking directly into the face of an angel — my Christmas Angel.